insight text guide

Sue Sciortino

Angela's Ashes

Frank McCourt

First published in 1999. Reprinted, with minor amendments, in 2019.

Insight Publications Pty Ltd
3/350 Charman Road
Cheltenham VIC 3192
Australia
Tel: +61 3 8571 4950
Fax: +61 3 8571 0257
Email: books@insightpublications.com.au

www.insightpublications.com.au

A catalogue record for this book is available from the National Library of Australia

Frank McCourt's Angela's Ashes / Sue Sciortino

ISBNs:
9781875882281 (print)
9781925485486 (digital)
9781925485516 (bundle: print + digital)

Cover design: Gisela Beer, based on a concept by The Modern Art Production Group

Printed in Australia

contents

CHARACTER MAP

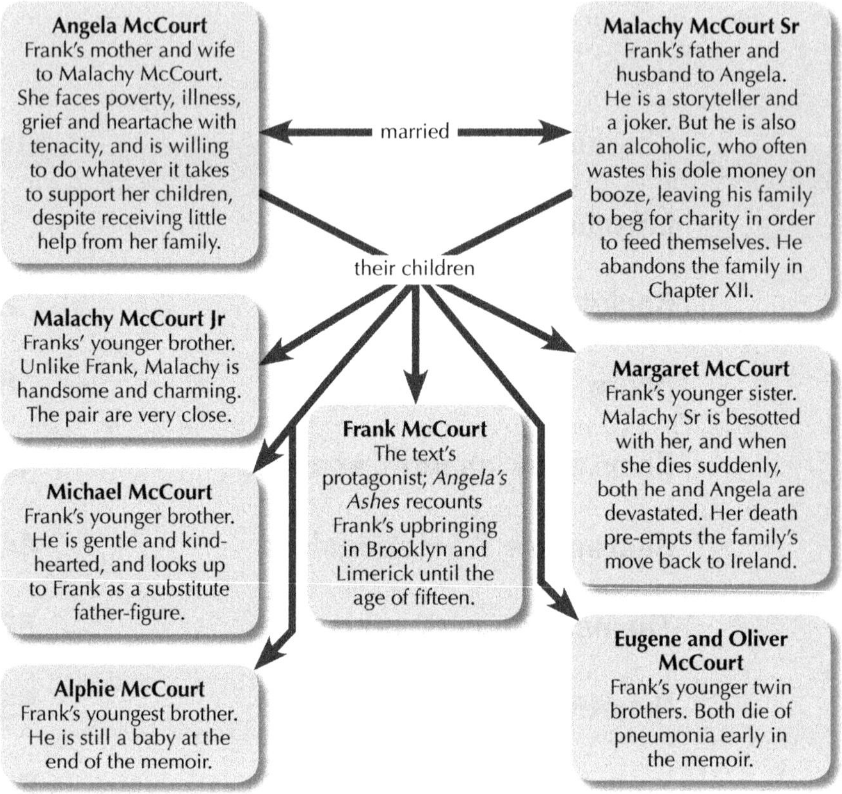

Angela McCourt
Frank's mother and wife to Malachy McCourt. She faces poverty, illness, grief and heartache with tenacity, and is willing to do whatever it takes to support her children, despite receiving little help from her family.

married

Malachy McCourt Sr
Frank's father and husband to Angela. He is a storyteller and a joker. But he is also an alcoholic, who often wastes his dole money on booze, leaving his family to beg for charity in order to feed themselves. He abandons the family in Chapter XII.

their children

Malachy McCourt Jr
Franks' younger brother. Unlike Frank, Malachy is handsome and charming. The pair are very close.

Frank McCourt
The text's protagonist; *Angela's Ashes* recounts Frank's upbringing in Brooklyn and Limerick until the age of fifteen.

Margaret McCourt
Frank's younger sister. Malachy Sr is besotted with her, and when she dies suddenly, both he and Angela are devastated. Her death pre-empts the family's move back to Ireland.

Michael McCourt
Frank's younger brother. He is gentle and kind-hearted, and looks up to Frank as a substitute father-figure.

Eugene and Oliver McCourt
Frank's younger twin brothers. Both die of pneumonia early in the memoir.

Alphie McCourt
Frank's youngest brother. He is still a baby at the end of the memoir.

Minor characters			
Agnes Sheehan	Laman Griffin	Margaret Sheehan	Mikey Molloy
Mr O'Halloran	Mr Timoney	Mrs Brigid Finucane	Pa Keating
Pat Sheehan (The Abbot)	Patricia Madigan	The Clohessys	Theresa Carmody

INTRODUCTION

Frank McCourt was born in America in 1930 to Irish immigrant parents. Winner of the 1997 Pulitzer Prize for Biography or Autobiography, *Angela's Ashes* records his early life and has become a bestseller, bringing international fame to this Irish-American retired English teacher.

As well as a memoir, the book is also a record of the social history of the urban poor in Ireland during the Great Depression. While life in America was also difficult in the 1930s, the McCourts' decision to immigrate back to Ireland was not a happy one. Immigration is one of the key themes in the book. Migrants often experience a mental dichotomy: 'home' is always the other country, the place where one aspires to be; home is a country of the mind. Children are desperate to fit in, but this is difficult for Frank who is 'a Yank' with a father from the Irish north suspected of Protestant leanings and having 'the odd manner'. The dream of returning to America and escaping the abject poverty of the Limerick slums colours Frank's life.

Angela's Ashes is characterised by the storytelling ability of the author, learned from his feckless, alcoholic father, who loves but does not provide for his children. Frank's life is presented starkly to the reader through a series of wryly humorous anecdotes, which reveal the harshness of authority and of the Irish Catholic Church, as well as the generosity of ordinary people. The story is one of a dysfunctional family that is quintessentially Irish.

The author explores the themes of innocence and experience, and the struggle for understanding and human development in a world in which survival is as much attributable to good luck as to adequate nurture.

BACKGROUND & CONTEXT

The Great Depression

The Great Depression was not just an economic crisis that swept the world; it quickly became a social one. It partially explains the poverty of the McCourts, especially in America – a country that had prospered economically since it gained independence in 1776. Frank was born in 1930, just as the impact of the 1929 stock market crash was beginning to bite. As companies became insolvent and banks closed their doors, unemployment became a scourge that swept the industrialised world. In Ireland, already an endemically poor nation, a long-running history of English oppression had dominated. By 1930 Ireland had not progressed far industrially and so there were few factories to provide work. Earlier policies preventing education meant, too, that the lowest strata of society were largely unskilled. Irish political policies, civil unrest and civil war in the south – the Irish Free State – exacerbated by the global economic crisis of the Great Depression, were major causes of extreme poverty in Ireland.

The Irish Question

The 'Irish Question' is the popular term for the entirety of Ireland's conflicts. It has proved to be one of the longest-running and most intractable issues in British politics, revolving around land and religion, and the causes extend far back in Ireland's troubled history.

The English king, Henry II, invaded Ireland in 1171 and brought Catholicism with him. In the thirteenth century, English settlers crossed to Ireland in their thousands and English courtiers became great landowners there, beginning a tradition of absentee landlordism. The Irish in the south were driven off the land into the poorest parts of the country, while in the north, the Irish were more successful in defending their lands. For centuries there have been rebellions and uprisings by the Irish against the English and, now, in the twenty-first century, there remains a longstanding rivalry.

English rule: Catholics and Protestants in Ireland

The history of English rule in Ireland is also bound up with Catholicism. When the Protestant Reformation swept England in the sixteenth century, it did not spread to Ireland and this proved to be a further source of conflict. England itself was to experience a turbulent period based on religious affiliation. By the close of the seventeenth century, Protestant holdings in Ireland had increased to eighty per cent. Under the Stuart rulers, William and Anne, in the late 1600s, a new set of repressive laws against Irish Catholics was enacted and for the next hundred years the Protestants monopolised power – until 1793.

Irish independence / Irish nationalism

The events of both the American Revolution (1776) and the French Revolution (1789) inspired calls for Irish independence. A rebellion was mounted in 1798. It failed, but played a formative part in the development of an Irish radical/revolutionary tradition. In 1800 William Pitt induced the Irish to vote its parliament out of existence; thus from 1801 the Act of Union established the United Kingdom of Great Britain and Ireland.

The economic development of Ireland was arrested. Consequently, a much-needed agrarian revolution did not take place. In 1845–47 the failure of the staple crop, the potato, on which the population largely depended, resulted in the Irish Famine, which led to widespread starvation among the Irish peasantry. Starvation and mass emigration meant that Ireland's population fell by an estimated twenty to twenty-five per cent.

With the land held by Protestant absentee landlords, Catholics (who made up three-quarters of the population) developed a movement of Irish nationalism. By the mid-nineteenth century, Ireland had representatives in the British Parliament and calls for 'Home Rule' (independence) became increasingly vociferous. Sinn Féin ('Ourselves Alone'), the Irish Nationalist Party, developed during 1905–08 to support Irish independence from Britain; other militant groups also formed. The famous Easter Rising of 1916 was a rebellion of Irish Nationalists in Dublin, organised by members of the Irish Republican Brotherhood and Sinn Féin. This insurrection was suppressed by British forces and its leaders executed, increasing sympathy for the nationalist cause in Ireland. In the Anglo-Irish War (1919–20), Britain attempted to coerce Ireland using armed police, regular soldiers and a vicious unit of recently demobbed soldiers known as the 'Black and Tans'. Irish nationalists formed the Irish Republican Army (IRA) in 1919 to oppose British forces in Ireland. It opposed the 1921 treaty that made Ireland a dominion and the six northern counties part of the United Kingdom. The IRA was suppressed in 1922, banned in 1936 by Eamon de Valera and remained largely inactive until the late 1960s.

A divided Ireland – Southern Ireland

Amid increasing violence, a proposal to divide Ireland was offered as a solution to the conflict. Although this was unacceptable to Sinn Féin, it was passed, ushering in the Irish Free State (the formal name for Southern Ireland). While Sinn Féin leader Michael Collins (also a founder and director of the IRA) accepted this arrangement, many other members of the IRA did not and a civil war followed in which Collins was killed in 1922. Frank is confused at school when he discovers that one teacher insists that Collins was the greatest man who ever lived while another claims that de Valera is (p.85) – as does his father Malachy, who reads *The Irish Press*, de Valera's newspaper (p.104).

In 1937 a new constitution established the Irish Free State as a sovereign state of the Commonwealth, and gave it the new name of Eire. In 1949 Eire withdrew from the Commonwealth and was re-named the Republic of Ireland. The IRA, however, continued to fight for an independent, unified Ireland with a campaign of violence – mainly in Northern Ireland and Britain.

Anti-Protestant feeling in *Angela's Ashes*

In the predominantly Catholic south there is strong anti-Protestant feeling, and this is evident in Limerick, the setting for most of *Angela's Ashes*. Angela's relatives suspect that Malachy McCourt, who is from the north, has Protestant origins. Frank, too, is troubled by his Presbyterian (a branch of Protestantism) hair and northern looks. Children chant the anti-Protestant schoolyard rhyme *'Proddy Woddy ring the bell, / Not for heaven but for hell'* (p.194), and Frank innocently reveals how the Catholic Church inculcates anti-Protestant attitudes:

> On Sunday mornings in Limerick I watch them go to church, the Protestants, and I feel sorry for them … they're doomed. That's what the priests tell us. Outside the Catholic Church there is no salvation. Outside the Catholic Church there is nothing but doom. And I want to save them. Protestant girl, come with me to the True Church. You'll be saved and you won't have the doom. (p.194)

Later, Frank experiences Mrs O'Connell's venom when he forsakes the post office to work for Easons: 'that pack of freemasons and Protestants above in Dublin' (p.396).

Northern Ireland

In contrast, Northern Ireland became mainly Protestant when, from 1921, the predominantly Protestant counties of Ulster withdrew from the newly formed Irish Free State with the signing of the Anglo-Irish Treaty. Furthermore, Northern Ireland continued under British rule, another divisive difference between the north and the south, seen in Mrs O'Connell's attitudes (quoted above).

As a result, in the north the Catholics were, and today still are, a minority. In the late 1960s, Protestant discrimination against Catholics in employment and housing resulted in spasmodic outbreaks of violence that the British were called upon to help quell. The IRA, based in Belfast, became extremely militant in 1969. A campaign of bombings, assassinations and attacks on troops and loyalists (Protestant sympathisers) sprang up in Northern Ireland and England, until finally attempts at peace were made.

Class and religion

The English class system was brought to Ireland with the English invasion. The very nature of absentee landlordism depended on a hierarchical social structure. The Catholic Church in Ireland, too, had its hierarchy and it was left to the lowest stratum of parish priests to administer to the poor. Organisations like the Jesuits and the Christian Brothers were concerned only with those above the poorest levels. Edward Royle, author of *Modern Britain: A Social History, 1750–1985*, suggests that, among the working classes, 'most churchgoers were hypocrites; the poor who did not go to church were the real Christians because they lived decently and helped their neighbours' (Royle 1989, p.334).

This was certainly the experience recorded by Frank McCourt. Royle goes on to explain: 'even the Catholic church was not entirely successful at maintaining its links with the Irish poor, despite common ties of culture and language between the priests and the people' (Royle 1989, p.334). Note that a priest never visits the McCourts and that their main link to the Church is through the school system.

Religion in *Angela's Ashes*

Formalised religion in *Angela's Ashes* is shown more as a means of social control, to keep the masses of the working poor in order. In their preparation for their first Holy Communion, moral and spiritual learning is inculcated through fear as the boys are drilled by the intolerant and old Mr Benson, who threatens to flog them 'till the blood spurts' (p.132) if they mention The Collection. In fact The Collection will buy a feast for these starving lads. Somehow, too, the parents have to buy the special apparel necessary for the occasion, something not questioned by Grandma, who is a pious Catholic. While there is some sign of charity, no meaningful steps are taken to redress the serious poverty that is so pervasive.

St. Vincent de Paul provides some help to Angela, but even there they have to collect heavy furniture themselves; watch that Mrs McGrath does not cheat them of their rightful amounts of flour, tea and so on; and be subject to inspection from suited representatives of the Church, who shake their heads and say 'God Almighty and Mother of God, this is desperate. That's not Italy they have upstairs, that's Calcutta' (p.114). There is no real help for Angela, who cannot stand in the queue for boots for the boys after the birth of a new baby: no exceptions are made.

However, a few teachers recognise Frank's obvious intellectual abilities, and try to stop discrimination against the poorer boys, showing a keen awareness of the impacts of poverty. See, for example, the instance when the class master threatens the boys if they sneer at the McCourts because their shoes have been clumsily mended with rubber from a car tyre (p.116). The accounts of the Church's demands and its limited charity, though, offer a bleak comment on the Irish Catholic Church during this period.

GENRE, STRUCTURE & STYLE

Genre

Angela's Ashes is a memoir written in first person that purports to be a record of the early life of the writer. Memoir draws on memory with all its errors, gaps and misapprehensions, and is quite distinct from the genre of biography, which is an account of someone's life written by somebody else. Biographies require a significant amount of research by the author, who seeks to produce an account that is as accurate, objective and reliable as possible. Frank McCourt, though writing about his own experiences, would also have checked as many primary sources as possible – the details of teachers at Leamy's National School, for example. Additionally, McCourt has dredged his own memory, and likely asked his relatives and other survivors of the period to confirm facts and dates.

Memoir draws on elements of fiction because events and incidents are specifically selected and placed in an order that may not be consecutive, but which is pleasing from a literary point of view. What McCourt presents is an account of his childhood and adolescence written after retirement. *Angela's Ashes* thus offers us Frank's viewpoint, his experiences and his interpretation of events. As such, it could be quite different from a memoir by someone else who went through similar experiences in Limerick in the late 1930s. It is Frank's subjective account of what happened and what he recollects of events. The intention of reproducing 'the truth' is there, but then the knotty question of what the truth really is arises.

First-person narration

The first-person narration is key to this work. The reader must decide, from the outset, whether the narrator – the adult Frank McCourt – is reliable or unreliable. As the story unfolds the reader decides whether the author is telling the truth and whether they can believe the child's experiences as filtered through the adult interpreter. As the book begins before the birth of the author, how can he be sure of the circumstances of his conception, for example? Indeed, part of the opening chapter is narrated from a third-person omniscient perspective, meaning that, while the story is still told in Frank's voice, he is able to reveal the thoughts and feelings of other characters as well as details about events he was not present for. The all-knowing position of the narrator here lends this account a ring of authenticity, whether the details are scrupulously related or not. The details of Frank McCourt's early life bear the tone of truthfulness, but it must be remembered that for most of the text he employs a limited point of view. Apart from the opening chapter, he cannot render more than his own emotions and memories; he can only interpret those of others.

Structure

In a memoir such as this, the writer relies on themes and motifs to draw the threads of the tale together. The major theme is growing up, and the linear progression of the story aids the development of this theme, as well as providing a stable structure through which Frank's life story evolves. In many ways the book can be viewed as a series of anecdotes, loosely strung together by first-person narration, but it is this anecdotal style that allows the writer to achieve the emotional range that he does. The reader is invited to laugh, to cry, to sympathise. There is shock and disgust and despair and bleakness. Above all, though, an overarching tenderness for Frank is evoked.

The book is split into two halves with Chapter VIII at the centre. The first half covers Frank's story from birth to age ten. The second half begins after the climax of the story, when Frank reaches the age of Confirmation in the Church, and covers events to the time he sails for New York. At the climax, Frank not only comes of age in the Church but also reaches an intellectual and emotional maturity. He reads his first Shakespearean passage, experiences comfort and cleanliness in the hospital, and is influenced by an inspirational teacher. Above all, he learns the power of the mind to conceal thoughts and emotions.

Cohering patterns, such as Malachy's alcoholic binges, are placed at strategic intervals to mark the ebb and flow of events. They underpin the authenticity of the tale and act as a structural device to meld the anecdotes together.

Language

The reader becomes engaged with the story because of the deceptive simplicity of the language and the poetic devices employed. In the scene where Frank contracts typhoid fever, for example, the author employs repetition of the words 'and I don't care' to convey Frank's complete loss of interest in what is happening around him. This device is used on several occasions to emphasise the narrator's intentions.

Ashes – an important motif

The symbol of the ashes is a significant cohering motif in the book. It has multiple interpretations.

- Frank's story rises from the ashes of Angela's life (like the mythical phoenix).
- Smoking Wild Woodbines (cigarettes) contributes to the poverty of the family.
- It is shorthand to convey that Angela is depressed.
- It represents the death of something (Angela and Malachy's marriage, for example).

- It points to the failure of expectations.
- The symbol of the ashes often appears at points of deep humiliation either for Angela or for Frank.

In an interview, the author has explained the circumstances of the distribution of Angela's cremated ashes (Lamb 1997); at Angela's request, they were taken to Ireland and scattered at a medieval abbey outside Limerick.

Style

Young Frank is loquacious: he has the gift of the gab. This is a reflection of the adult author's narrative style, learned from his storytelling father. The style is unmistakably Irish, with a persuasive charm that convinces the reader of Frank's innate humanity in the face of inhuman conditions. It is that traditionally Irish gift for, and love of, language that allows McCourt to survive with so little bitterness, and to render his account with so little sentimentality. But the style has American undertones, too. It is sharp and economical and, although his father and mother fit the stereotypical Irish character types – the alcoholic, errant father; the defeated, despairing mother – they are portrayed, without sentiment, as endearingly human. Importantly, there are no clichés in this book. Malachy is not a villain, he is merely flawed, helpless and hopeless.

If you are at times overwhelmed by the bleakness of the daily life portrayed by McCourt, on a second reading try allowing the humour to surface, so that the reading can become an uplifting experience – at its heart, it is a story of survival, a survival of the human spirit.

CHAPTER-BY-CHAPTER ANALYSIS

Chapter I (pp.1–43)

Summary: *Father's background: a farm in Ireland's north (pp.2–3); mother's background (pp.3–5); Frank's parents meet in New York, birth and baptism of Frank (p.9); pattern of father's behaviour set.*

The opening paragraphs set the tone of the book. The second paragraph is much quoted by reviewers because it is an accurate preview of what Frank is to relate about his childhood in Limerick, Ireland. The father, Malachy McCourt, grew up in Northern Ireland and escaped, after fighting with the IRA, to America as a wanted man. The mother, Angela Sheehan, from the Limerick slums, has a brother, Uncle Pat, who has an acquired brain injury, the fault of his father. Angela proves to be 'useless' (p.5) and her intolerant mother pays her fare to America. There she meets Malachy and becomes pregnant.

Already, the author's anecdotal style is evident as he relates each passage – note the humorous story recounting how Malachy came to be in jail in the months prior to meeting Angela (p.5). Angela's large, unsympathetic cousins, the MacNamara sisters, take steps to ensure that Malachy does 'the right thing' (p.7). The unsuitability of the husband is less important than the social disgrace of having a child out of wedlock. He decides to escape to San Francisco but, typically, he drinks away his escape money and, four months after the wedding, Francis (named after his grandfather and also St. Francis) is born. The cousins caution Angela against further pregnancies, since Malachy does not have a job and 'he drinks' (p.11). Note the change in narration (p.3) to an omniscient narrator.

From the first-person narrative perspective, Frank constructs his childhood in a tenement in Brooklyn. He is three. His brother Malachy is two, and Frank's first recollections are of causing injury to Malachy on the seesaw and of his mother's continual pregnancies.

Frank's father is revealed early as a storyteller, as he regales Frank with the great Celtic myths of the deeds of Cuchulain (pp.12–13). Importantly, in these scenes Frank is shown as being very comfortable with his father. The contrast between the two older brothers is drawn here: while Malachy is fair with an engaging smile, Frank is dark and has 'the odd manner' of his father (p.14). The indigence of the father is first demonstrated here, for when there are wages 'we know the weekend will be wonderful', there will be food and 'Dad tells us a story out of his head' (p.16). Angela sings. This lasts only for two weeks and then Malachy gets drunk on his wages. There is no food, and when he returns late at night he gets the boys up to sing patriotic songs of Ireland. The next week Angela tries to intercept his wages but Malachy loses his job and blames her. The pattern of their lives is set. It never changes, and how the family survives the kind of poverty inflicted upon them forms the body of the book.

Key point

The author relates the family's hardships with humour and a surprising lack of bitterness. Things are the way they are and it is better to laugh at oneself than be subsumed by anger and resentment.

Angela is often depressed: a depression not alleviated either by the birth of twin boys or of a daughter, Margaret. Malachy is charmed, almost obsessed by his fragile daughter, but Angela is overwhelmed by the birth of five children in four years, by lack of an income and by Malachy's alcoholism. She is unable to cope. The twins are rarely clean and are fed mostly sugar and water. Here, Frank finds he is capable of stealing food for himself and his brothers (p.26).

Throughout the book the harshness of their lives is leavened by the simple kindnesses of others, usually in similar circumstances to themselves. In this chapter note the help rendered by the MacAdoreys and the Leibowitzes (pp.3–40), as well as by the Italian grocer. By contrast, in later chapters, both their relations and the rich are characterised by their meanness.

Frank begins to notice differences in culture and language, which help him to refine his picture of himself as measured against others (p.29), and begins to develop an imagination. When the baby Margaret dies, Frank's parents are distraught and each handle the event in their own characteristic way: Angela takes to her bed in deep depression, while Malachy gets drunk. Frank not only does not understand the hysteria exhibited by Angela in her grief, but is left with the responsibility of caring for himself and his brothers, when the young twins do not even have clean nappies, only rags (p.34). The neighbours take charge and, eventually, the callous cousins write to Ireland for money to send the family back.

Key point

The book is like a woven tapestry with patterns repeating at spaced intervals. In this first chapter several motifs are introduced that recur throughout: Malachy's alcoholism and the consequent hardships, Angela's depression signified by 'ashes', the repressive nature of authority and the humanity of ordinary people.

Q What is the significance of storytelling in this opening chapter? What role does storytelling play in Frank's relationship with his father?

Q How does McCourt establish a sense of time and place in this opening chapter? What is your sense of the community in which the McCourts are living?

Chapter II (pp.44–97)

Summary: *Neither side of the family takes them in (pp.47 & 57); the twins die (pp.77–8 & 87); Angela moves the family several times (p.78); Frank and his brother Malachy start school (p.83); their father goes on the dole and Angela seeks church 'charity' (pp.82 & 64–9); introduction of Grandma (p.55), Aunt Aggie and Pa Keating (p.58).*

The family returns to Ireland, penniless, and the cycle of poverty, alcoholism and rejection by relatives continues. The return to the father's place in the north is a disaster for 'things are worse here than they are in

America' (p.47), so the family is bundled onto a bus bound for Dublin, where it is hoped that Malachy will be provided with a pension for his IRA work. This is denied, partly because of his alcoholism. They are destitute at the station but, out of kindness, the police pay their fares to Limerick (p.54), where the family hopes Angela's mother will take them in. She is another of the sour-faced relations who, together with Aunt Aggie, endeavour to make their lives as difficult as possible. She has no room because she cares for the brain-damaged Uncle Pat, but she does pay the first rent for a furnished room for them in Windmill Street, the first of their residences in the Lanes of Limerick. The children are happy again after the hardships they have endured since leaving Brooklyn: 'it didn't matter that there were six of us in the bed, we were together, away from grandmothers and guards ... and we could laugh as much as we liked', despite 'the fleas leaping, jumping, fastened to our flesh' in the bed (p.59).

Key point

This is the essence of the family's relationships with each other. No matter how poor or hungry they are, there is love rather than repression. Irish Catholicism is introduced early and becomes an inescapable part of their lives, underlining the differences between the love in the family and the harshness of authority outside.

Uncle Pa Keating is a simple man with a cough, probably emphysema, contracted from inhaling German gas in World War I. He proves to be sympathetic; however, he is mostly ineffectual in overriding his wife (Aunt Aggie) or the children's grandmother.

Angela loses a baby and Frank is mystified; the adults never explain anything to the children.

Malachy goes to the Labour Exchange for the dole, which is not enough to provide for the children, and this prompts the first instance of Angela looking 'into the ashes'; 'you can see the worry where the corners of her mouth turn down' (p.64). This is a running symbol through the book, used to accentuate, in particular, moments of humiliation caused either to Angela or to Frank. Here, it presages her first encounter with the 'charity' of the Church's St. Vincent de Paul Society, whose minions threaten the loss of religious deserters' immortal souls for they are 'doomed to the deepest part of hell' (p.66). Later this oft-repeated threat causes Frank to ponder on the nature of the 'doom', which seems inescapable. Angela receives a coupon to use at a designated shop where the owner is notorious for cheating the poor.

Oliver becomes ill and the consequent behaviour of both parents reveals their ignorance and inability to care for the children. Malachy is given their coal docket to make a fire for the sick child, but when the coal yards are closed he refuses to collect coal from the side of the road, saying, 'we're not beggars' (p.71). This reveals the misguided pride that characterises him throughout the book. He is, however, not too proud to beg for 'a pint'. In portraying the character with such double standards, McCourt encourages readers to lose respect for him here, and perhaps for the rest of the story. Angela is not so proud but realises too late the seriousness of Oliver's illness, and he dies, probably of malnutrition and pneumonia. The other children are taken to Aunt Aggie's, where even the grandmother is appalled at Aggie's meanness, which stems from resentment that Angela produces children without effort while she is barren (p.76). Malachy spends the dole money on drink again, his excuse this time being that he is grieving for Oliver and Margaret. At this point the reader despairs at Malachy's negligence and Angela's 'uselessness'.

In grief, Angela moves house again, this time to Hartstonge Street, their second Lane address (p.82). The parents ensure that Frank and his brother Malachy start school. They understand the principles of education as both of them have had some schooling and realise that, for their children, it is the key to escaping poverty. The boys are initiated into the hardships of a basic education that emphasises the value of corporal punishment:

> they all have leather straps, canes, blackthorn sticks ... They hit you if you're late, if you have a leaky nib on your pen, if you laugh, if you talk, and if you don't know things.

> They hit you if you don't know why God made the world, if you don't know the patron saint of Limerick ... if you can't add nineteen to forty-seven, if you can't subtract nineteen from forty-seven ... (p.84)

Note the author's use of repetition, a poetic device he uses throughout the book, to reinforce his points.

The loss of Oliver is particularly poignant as we see his twin, Eugene, longing for his brother and fretting over his absence. Despite his brothers' best endeavours, Eugene also dies. It would seem his death is caused by pneumonia (and probably malnutrition) but the author makes it appear to be a result of the loss of his twin. The reader again rails at the ignorance and neglect of the parents.

Key point

The detail of Malachy's alcoholic binge with Eugene's coffin is extremely funny when one puts aside, as the reader is meant to do, the sorrow of the occasion (pp.92–3). This is a typical example of how the sombreness of the story is relieved by humour. The fact that Frank is there as an observer lends credibility to the incident. Frank's internal repetition of the phrase 'I don't know why ...' (p.95) captures the innocence and wonder of the child persona.

Q Write a brief comparison (a few paragraphs) of life in the Brooklyn tenement and life in the Limerick Lanes. In what ways do the events of Chapter I foreshadow Frank's experiences in Ireland?

Q What are your first impressions of Aunt Aggie?

Chapter III (pp.98–123)

Summary: *Life in Roden Lane: Italy upstairs, Ireland downstairs (p.104); Christmas dinner (p.110); the Angel on the Seventh Step (p.111).*

The family's move to Roden Lane cements the cycle of alcoholism, unemployment, pregnancy, charity and destitution. The new quarters in Roden Lane appear, at first, to be an improvement, but they soon find that the lavatory next door is a communal one for the whole street, which contaminates their premises. The author's humorous writing style, which lightens the account of their impoverished lifestyle, is established in this chapter where matters such as the lavatory are treated comically.

There are several memorable scenes here. The living quarters become flooded in winter, so the family moves upstairs. The upstairs area, offering warmth and comfort, is dubbed 'Italy', while downstairs, only habitable in the summer, remains 'Ireland' (p.104). References to 'Italy' and 'Ireland' occur throughout the rest of their occupation of Roden Lane. Another recurring image is that of the picture of the Pope that has been transported from America. The disastrous attempt to 'hang' the picture typifies how the wretchedness of their lives is relieved by humour (p.100).

The dole is reduced upon the death of the twins, but Malachy does not work. He seeks odd jobs on outlying farms, but regards that as his money: 'he takes the farm money to the pub and drinks it' (p.102). He returns home singing and gets the children up to 'promise to die for Ireland' (p.103). Angela 'hopes he might bring home something from the farm, potatoes, cabbage, turnips, carrots, but he'll never ... stoop so low as to ask a farmer for anything' (pp.102–3). While it is all right for Angela to beg at the St. Vincent de Paul Society, 'he says it's different for a man. You have to keep the dignity' (p.103). Young Frank clearly does not understand this male chauvinism or Malachy's advice that 'when you grow up you have to wear a collar and tie and never let people see you carry things' (p.107).

It is Christmas and Angela hopes for something nice, like a goose, for their dinner, but all they can obtain is a 'pig's head', which Frank is left to carry. Angela is humiliated and fears the neighbours seeing their paltry dinner, but Frank feels sorry for the pig 'because he's dead and the world is laughing at him' (p.106). When there is no coal for the fire to cook the pig, Frank and his brother Malachy engage in an amusing but sad struggle to bring back some coal:

> It takes us a long time to go ... because of a hole in the bag. I pull the bag and it's Malachy's job to pick up the lumps that fall through the hole and put them back again ... (p.109)

And it is there that they encounter rejection and humiliation with a hint of racism. The children are covered in black dust from the coal and, from a nearby shop, a woman calls to them to 'get away from that door, 'tis Christmas Day and she doesn't want to be looking at Africa' (p.109).

Angela gives birth to Michael, and Malachy creates a special story for Frank, who is aged no more than five: 'Dad says he found Michael on the seventh step of the stairs to Italy' (p.111). This becomes the place where Frank develops his imagination, creating dreams and pondering the nature of his existence over the next few years, consulting the Angel as his confidant. Humour is built up around Frank's childhood observances: the children need new shoes, so Malachy repairs them with a bicycle tyre: 'the tire pieces are so lumpy we stumble when we walk around Italy' (p.115). The image created is most amusing, but Frank feels 'ashamed'.

Young Frank accepts the life of the unemployed men as 'normal' but the adult Frank/narrator shows a touch of cynicism (p.118). When his father gets a job at the cement factory, Angela is optimistic and attempts to clean. The question here to be pondered is why she exhibits such naive optimism. Frank, the reader and the whole neighbourhood know that the cycle of alcoholism and unemployment will continue, and this is emphasised by the narrator when he compares their situation with that of other poor families (p.120). Again, Angela is disappointed and 'lies in her bed with Michael in her arms ... I can hear her crying' (pp.121–2). The desperation of the 'ashes' symbolism is evoked here as Malachy returns drunk, singing 'Roddy McCorley'.

Q 'A man without collar and tie is a man with no respect for himself' (p.102). What is your impression of Malachy McCourt from this chapter? Is he a respectable man? Why or why not?

Chapter IV (pp.124–45)

Summary: *Mikey Molloy and his family (pp.124–7); Frank is coached for his first Holy Communion (pp.127–32); The Collection (p.131); First Confession (p.140).*

Frank at seven is now expected to die for the Faith as well as for Ireland. The confusion in his young mind gives rise to great amusement: 'I don't think I'll live that long the way I'm expected to die for this or that' (p.124). A long anecdote about Mikey Molloy is inserted here. He is older than Frank and has already experienced First Communion. He is subject to fits but provides Frank with some idea of how things will be through his experience as 'the expert in the lane on Girls' Bodies and Dirty Things in General' (p.125).

School consists of religion administered through fear and corporal punishment. Interwoven is an anecdote of a boy even worse off than Frank. Paddy Clohessy's father has 'consumption' (tuberculosis) and Frank is generous towards him (p.133). Mikey's father is unemployed and brings home books from the library, which the boys read. Mikey tells Frank an irreverent story about his hero Cuchulain, whose wife 'was the champion woman pisser of Ireland' (p.137). Mikey then tells Frank that by listening to this story he has committed a sin and must tell the priest at his First Confession. Frank is perplexed but his confession is most amusing to the priest who hears it (pp.140–1).

Frank does not know why his First Communion day is supposed to be the 'happiest day of his life' (p.141). First he is scrubbed red raw by his grandmother, who is piously religious. Although there is never enough money for food, a suit still has to be provided, and Frank is late because he has 'standing up, North of Ireland, Presbyterian hair' (p.143). He nearly misses the occasion and finds it difficult to swallow the wafer.

One bright spot in the life of a small Catholic boy in Limerick is 'The Collection' that takes place after the ceremony, when the boys go from house to house receiving sweets and money to visit the cinema. After

Frank's First Communion, Grandma provides a breakfast which Frank vomits up. She is furious because she believes the wafer, the body of Christ, has also been regurgitated and now she has 'God in me backyard' (p.143). She takes him to Confession and, again, the priest is convulsed with laughter at Frank's sin (p.144). She forbids Frank to make The Collection but Angela stands up for him and he sneaks into the cinema after Mikey creates a diversion (p.145).

Key point

The humour in this chapter, as so often in the book, is derived from the juxtaposition of Frank's innocence against adult behaviour.

Q What does the anecdote about Paddy Clohessy and the raisin tell us about Frank's character?

Q What is the significance of Angela standing up to her mother in order to allow Frank to make The Collection and visit the cinema?

Chapter V (pp.146–67)

Summary: *Father shown as much more literate than others (p.149); Frank's brother Malachy gets false teeth stuck (pp.154–5); Frank is sent to dancing lessons (p.155); Frank joins the Confraternity (pp.162–5); rejection as altar boy (p.167).*

In this chapter, Frank is shown as less than perfect. He lies, spends precious money and eats Grandma's boarder's food. He is a thoroughly normal, lovable seven-year-old. His life unfolds against a background of Irish politics where people feud because of their political positions, or because they have connections with the hated English (p.146) or because they are are 'soupers' (p.147).

Frank's grandmother's extreme devoutness is contrasted with her meanness and hypocrisy (pp.149–50). She takes in a Protestant boarder – although she hates Protestants – simply because he pays. She does not see this as compromising her religious principles although Frank /

the narrator does. Frank is paid to take the boarder's dinner to him, but is so hungry he eats it himself. It is Angela who is punished for this sinful behaviour because Frank must now deliver the dinner for free (pp.151–3).

The Wild Woodbines (cigarettes) play a vital role in the lives of the McCourts. Although there is no money for food, both parents smoke (p.153) and, consequently, their teeth rot prematurely and have to be extracted. The replacement false teeth are the source of a hilarious anecdote about Frank's brother Malachy inserting his father's new set and having to be taken to hospital to have them removed (pp.154–5).

Angela decides that Frank should learn Irish dancing and become rich and famous. He is given sixpence every Saturday for his lessons, but Frank is so embarrassed by his friends thinking he is 'sissy', he decides to spend the money at the Lyric Cinema instead. Of course, he is discovered and dragged off to Confession by his father, not so much for stealing the money as for his lack of patriotism.

Now Frank is 'seven, eight, nine going on ten' (p.161). Note the way the author progresses the narrative by using the present tense. Circumstances have not changed. Malachy is still feckless and the family is still poor. Malachy buys drinks for men who boost his ego, needing to be thought of as brave and grand (p.162).

Frank is persuaded to join the Confraternity, a religious organisation that recruits boys and keeps them in line through fear (pp.162–5). Malachy decides that Frank should become an altar boy and prepares him well, but the door is shut in his face because he is from a poor family (p.167). This is a crucial moment for Frank; it will not be the only time the Church rejects him due to his impoverishment.

Key point

In this chapter Frank's parents' higher literacy ensures they want, and expect, a better life for him. His father 'has a lovely way with the English language and a fine fist for the writing' (p.149), his mother reads poetry and later Frank is taught Latin. From First Communion onwards, though, Frank's life moves outside mere parental influence.

Q Discuss the examples of religious hypocrisy in this chapter.

Chapter VI (pp.168–90)

Summary: *Maths at school (pp.168–72); education laced with religion (pp.172–4); Fintan the homosexual (pp.174–80); wagging school (pp.180–3); Paddy Clohessy (pp.173–84); Dennis Clohessy and Angela (pp.184–90); Frank's peer group becomes important.*

In the fourth class, Frank learns geometry from Mr O'Neill. Mr O'Neill tortures the boys, who are all poor, with the apple he peels in front of them every day. Fintan Slattery, a boy favoured by Mr O'Neill, receives the peelings as a reward for knowing who stood at the foot of the cross when Jesus was crucified (pp.173–5). The classroom hierarchy is evident in these scenes: Frank dreads being associated with Fintan (p.173), just as Brendan Quigley (also known as 'Question') fears his reputation as 'the master's pet' (p.170).

Fintan Slattery is portrayed as a pious boy who obeys the Christian ideal to the letter. He pretends friendship and kindness to Frank and Paddy Clohessy and invites them home for lunch. The boys think he is going to share his lunch with them as he is well provided for by his even more pious mother. Although they are afraid of his homosexual advances towards them they are so hungry they go with him, but he too tortures the boys with food by cutting his sandwich into tiny sections and then eating them one by one, without offering the boys any (p.179). With his lack of generosity, Fintan provides yet another example of a character whose supposed Christian values are not reflected in their actual behaviour.

Frank and Paddy decide to skip school because they have missed out on lunch and are hungry. They go to an orchard to pick apples and stuff themselves, then drink milk straight from a cow. It is a delightful scene, the language clearly conveying their pleasure, not just in eating stolen food, but in the rare occasion of appeasing their hunger: 'I'm wondering why anyone should be hungry in a world full of milk and apples' (p.180).

The boys get caught in a storm but are happy until Frank finds out his parents are out looking for him for skipping school. In a panic he goes to Paddy's house where the poverty is even more evident than it is at Frank's. Although he is afraid of catching tuberculosis from Paddy's father in the unhealthy conditions, he stays the night. When Angela comes for him with the Guard in the morning, Paddy's father realises she is a friend from his youth and, although he is ill, Angela takes pity on him and sings for him, remembering a happy episode in her life. In her shock at seeing Dennis Clohessy, she forgets to punish Frank for his truancy. Frank is thankful but feels 'very sorry for the Clohessys and all their troubles' (p.190).

Q The episode with the Clohessys show that there are families in the Lanes even worse off than the McCourts. Discuss how this passage (pp.184–90) contributes to the themes of the text.

Chapter VII (pp.191–210)

Summary: *Frank is nine and has gained a confused knowledge of Irish history (p.191); Protestant/Catholic antipathy is carefully interwoven with the narrative; Frank works for Uncle Pat (pp.194–7); Mr Timoney widens Frank's world (pp.196–202).*

Frank questions the need to die for Ireland: 'men have been dying for Ireland since the beginning of time and look at the state of the country' (p.191). He is becoming analytical in his thinking and able to sort out ideas for himself. He better understands the relationship between his parents and the increasing strain within it.

The anecdote about Mickey Spellacy, 'whose relations are dropping one by one of the galloping consumption' (p.192), is placed here to show that the concerns of the children in the Lanes revolve around food: the lack of it and the need for it. Frank envies Spellacy, who is given money and sweets by the folk of the Lanes to ease his 'sorrow', and who brags of the 'ham and cheese and cake and sherry and lemonade' on offer at his family members' wakes (p.193).

Frank is concerned for the lovely Protestant girls whom he watches walk to Church every Sunday morning. It has been drummed into him by the priests that everyone who is not Catholic is 'doomed', and he wants to save these girls with their 'beautiful white teeth', who laugh and play croquet, apparently unaware of their imminent damnation (p.194).

Grandma persuades Angela that it is time for Frank to earn a few pennies by helping Uncle Pat deliver his newspapers. Pat is selfish and exploits Frank as slave labour, buying fish and chips for himself and nothing for Frank. Although Frank has done all the work, he is only paid threepence while Uncle Pat spends one shilling on his dinner. Nevertheless, delivering the papers gives Frank the chance to meet Mr Timoney, who offers to pay Frank for reading to him, as his sight is failing.

Key point

This is a crucial part of Frank's development. He is to read from a collection of Jonathan Swift – not the well-known *Gulliver's Travels* but a shorter piece, 'A Modest Proposal', that satirises the condition of children in Ireland. 'A Modest Proposal' suggests solving part of the Irish Problem by cooking Irish babies.

Angela is pleased at Frank's new job but misunderstands the nature of Swift's political satire: 'that's all right, 'tis only a children's book' (p.198). The relationship is good for Frank because Mr Timoney is an educated anti-Catholic and becomes Frank's confidant. Unfortunately, Mr Timoney is taken to the City Home, where they keep 'old people who are helpless or demented' (p.201). Frank knows Mr Timoney is not mad, but the story of how his dog 'bit the postman, the milkman and a passing nun' (p.201) is amusing. Frank will miss his sixpence, but it is not the money that drives him to try to see Mr Timoney, it is his innate kindness.

Angela has another baby, Alphie, and although Frank's knowledge of the outside world is widening, he is still ignorant about sexual matters. When Frank's father gets drunk on the five pounds Grandpa in the north sends for the new baby, Frank's faith in him is irretrievably lost. Frank and his brother Malachy search every pub in Limerick but cannot find him. Frank is starving and eats the fish and chips belonging to a drunk and feels guilty. He goes to Confession and the priest is shocked by the level of Frank's destitution, but the child Frank does not understand why (pp.208–9). The narrator (adult Frank) understands clearly, enhancing the reader's knowledge of the relationship between the Church and its congregation. He shows that the parish priest appreciates the hardships of the poor but can do little to alleviate their conditions, for it seems the Church believes in the adage 'God helps those who help themselves'. Malachy and Angela do not try to help themselves.

Frank feels impotent with rage when he finds his father and he knows that from that point on 'it will be different'; 'it's bad enough to drink the dole or the wages but a man that drinks the money for a new baby is gone beyond the beyonds as my mother would say' (p.210).

Q Explain Mr Timoney's role in Frank's development.

Q Frank rarely blames his father for the hardships his family encounters, but his perception of his father begins to alter here. How does the use of language in this chapter reflect the development of characters and relationships?

Key point

There is a subtle change in Frank and Malachy's relationship from this point on. In a recent interview Frank speaks about his father in an impassive tone, stemming perhaps from the realisation that his father just did not care; he left them to starve (Lamb 1997).

Chapter VIII (pp.211–45)

Summary: *Frank's Confirmation (p.214); he contracts typhoid fever (pp.215–18); he reads his first Shakespeare (p.221–2); has an inspirational teacher (pp.235–7); regret tinges his love for his father (pp.237–9). This chapter is the climax of the book, where Frank becomes more adult and learns the power of the mind to conceal.*

Frank is ten and must be prepared for his Confirmation. He is told by the master that he will be prepared to die for the Faith:

> Confirmation means you're a true soldier of the Church and that entitles you to die and be a martyr in case we're invaded by Protestants or Mahommedans or any other class of a heathen. More dying. I want to tell them I won't be able to die for the Faith because I'm already booked to die for Ireland. (p.211)

Although young Frank is serious in his concerns, adult Frank / the narrator is able to convey the wry humour of Frank's anxiety and to accentuate his youth in comparison with Mikey Molloy's superior knowledge: ''tis only a saying they made up to frighten you ... All the dying is done' (p.211). Besides, Frank is not ready to die yet because he has another chance at The Collection.

In order for Frank to have a sin to confess, Peter Dooley (Quasimodo) arranges for him to peep at his sisters' naked bodies, for a fee (pp.212–13). Mikey, now fourteen, is a regular patron and pays a shilling to take a look. In climbing up the pipe he falls and later it is revealed that the fall cures his fits. Angela is horrified that perhaps Frank's sin is so bad he will not be able to wear the suit she has saved for all year. (They are starving but still the ceremonial gear must be provided for the Church.)

Frank makes his Confirmation anyway, but his nose starts bleeding and he feels ill:

> there is hugging and kissing in the bright sun and I don't care. My father is working and I don't care. My mother kisses me and I don't care. The boys talk about The Collection and I don't care. (p.215)

Again, note the careful use of repetition by the author here to encapsulate the child's feelings. Frank must be seriously ill, because he is prepared to miss The Collection.

The medical ignorance of the parents and grandmother is shown again here, together with the incompetence of a drunken doctor (p.216), underlining the fragility of life in Ireland at this time. Eventually, Frank is rushed to hospital with typhoid fever: a bacterial infection characterised by intestinal inflammation and ulceration. He is given both a transfusion and Extreme Unction, so that even in his feverish state he realises that he might die. He passes the crisis by the power of 'prayer', according to Sister Rita, an uncompromising, insensitive representative of both the Church and the medical profession. Frank is touched by the visit of his father who 'kisses me on the forehead for the first time in my life' (p.218). At this unusual demonstration of affection, Frank is 'so happy I feel like floating out of the bed' (p.218). He has not only been starved bodily, but starved for affection as well.

In the next room is Patricia Madigan, a girl suffering from diphtheria, but the two children are not allowed to meet, more because they are of a different sex than because they are suffering from different infectious diseases. Seamus, the hospital cleaner, acts as a go-between and brings Frank a short history of England to read. Thus, through Seamus, Patricia gives Frank something priceless: his first reading of Shakespeare, 'and it's like having jewels in my mouth when I say the words' (p.222). She teaches Frank a poem, 'The Highwayman' by Alfred Noyes, but when the Sister finds out they have been talking, she banishes Frank to another floor, where he is isolated from human company before he can learn the last stanzas of the poem. Through Sister Rita the author again shows the unrelenting harshness of authority. Patricia dies but, again, the kindness of ordinary people is emphasised when Seamus learns the last of the poem in the pub. He cannot read but learns to recite it so Frank can hear the end of the poem (p.227).

The 'girl in the blue dress' brings him leftover books to read and Frank's world is transformed: 'it's lovely to know the world can't interfere with the inside of your head'; 'I can dream about the red-lipped landlord's daughter and the highwayman, and the nurses and nuns can do nothing about it' (p.229).

Key point

This is a crucial passage because Frank has not only developed his imagination but has also learned the power of the mind to conceal. From this point he knows that no-one can read his thoughts and that he can create a world in his head that he does not have to share.

Frank spends his eleventh birthday in hospital without visitors. After fourteen weeks he is allowed home to rest and to eat 'beef' to build up his strength. The irony of that prescription is apparent to the reader, who knows that no such thing as beef has ever been available to the family. Frank cannot help but compare his home situation with his time in the hospital, and now knows there is something better to be sought after in life:

> I lie in bed and think of the hospital where the white sheets were changed every day and there wasn't a sign of a flea. There was a lavatory where you could sit and read your book ... There was a bath where you could sit in hot water as long as you liked [and quote Shakespeare] ... (p.231)

When Frank returns to school, he has missed so many classes that he is put back a grade. He is humiliated by being in the same class as his younger brother, especially when he already knows the work. He is so desperate to get out of the class, in his weakened condition, he staggers to St. Francis's church to light a candle and pray for a return to sixth class. The master wants to show off how much Frank learned from him last year and asks him to write a composition on 'Our Lord'. Frank's report, 'Jesus and the Weather', is comical but offers more social comment on the bleakness of life in Limerick than reflection about God. It is a logical, analytical piece, which most impresses the master. He is returned to the sixth class.

Through his elevation to sixth class, Frank meets Mr O'Halloran, a teacher who 'tells us what is important and why' (p.236). For the first time he is exposed to the knowledge of someone who is educated and prepared to explain even such things as 'cruelty on both sides' in the English/Irish conflicts. After what Frank has learned earlier, he finds it difficult to believe Mr O'Halloran but, with childish faith, knows his teacher could not tell a lie because he is the headmaster.

Above all, Mr O'Halloran teaches the importance of knowledge as a basis for forming an opinion:

> You have to study and learn so that you can make up your own mind ... but you can't make up an empty mind. Stock your mind ... It is your house of treasure and no one in the world can interfere with it. (p.236)

Frank takes this advice to heart.

A passage follows on Frank's father, which shows the boy's mature understanding. He recognises that his father does bad things – 'he drinks the dole money', causing Angela 'to beg at the St. Vincent de Paul Society' (p.237) – but Frank loves him regardless. After all, he is the storyteller and the creator of the 'Angel on the Seventh Step', the one who shares his knowledge with Frank. He tells him about one of the deepest sins the English committed against the Irish: 'the English wouldn't let the Catholics have schools because they wanted to keep the people ignorant' (p.238), a strategy of many conquering nations through history. The 'Catholic children met in hedge schools in the depths of the country' because the people 'loved learning' and 'the masters risked their lives going from ditch to ditch and hedge to hedge' in fear of being caught and sentenced to transportation (p.238). Malachy endeavours to give Frank an appreciation of his own history, which helps Frank to envision a future for himself in America: 'I'll go back to America and get an inside job ...

I'll be in out of the rain and I'll have a suit and shoes and a warm place to live' (p.238).

Key point

There is a transition here: while Frank appreciates what his father has given him, he also begins to reject and denounce Malachy for his inability to provide for and support his family. In the next chapter Malachy leaves and does not play a substantial role in their lives again.

At the end of this chapter, we move from the education of the mind to life on the physical level. Three anecdotes focus on the material world: the disgraceful lavatory in the Lane (pp.239–41); Frank's Christmas dinner at the hospital (pp.242–4), a striking contrast to another family pig's head dinner; and the death of Finn the horse (pp.244–5). These emphasise the growing gap between the pleasures of the mind and the physical degradation in which Frank finds himself.

Q How does Frank's time in the hospital contribute to his intellectual development?

Q Read Frank's composition on page 234. What does it reveal about life in Limerick?

Q What makes Mr O'Halloran such an inspirational figure for Frank?

Chapter IX (pp.246–68)

Summary: *A new kind of poverty divide (pp.246–8); Malachy leaves for work in England (pp.248–52); Frank contracts conjunctivitis (pp.256–7); the family fail to receive a telegram (pp.255–6); Mr Kane humiliates Angela (pp.267–8).*

The Limerick men are leaving for England, where there is plenty of work in the factories to help the war effort. Angela and Malachy's relationship has deteriorated; Angela does not want more children while Malachy expects 'the good Catholic woman [to] perform her wifely duties and submit to her husband or face eternal damnation' (p.246). Nevertheless, Malachy succumbs to family pressure and goes to Coventry. The family's hopes are high because the other men who have left send back their wages and their families are much better off. This is a new era of the 'haves' and 'have nots', a social divide underscored by the arrival of the telegram boys on Saturdays, who bring notification of remittances (p.246).

Angela is sad at Malachy's departure, perhaps sensing that this is the end of their relationship, and 'turns away to look into the ashes' (p.249), presaging the disappointment they all feel when their great expectations of receiving abundant amounts of money are not met. Thus with Malachy's departure, the family becomes far worse off, now completely dependent on the harsh charity meted out by the authorities. 'The Relief' is far worse than 'the dole'; it is all there is for deserted families.

Adult Frank / the narrator spells out the humiliation the desperate women suffer in order to obtain basic subsistence (p.256), something that the young Frank could not have appreciated as keenly as the adult.

Frank contracts conjunctivitis, which Grandma says is a result of too much reading, and he is taken to the Dispensary: the place 'where the poor people see doctors' (p.257). Frank is sent to hospital where, again, he is subjected to authoritarian rule without reason: 'I try to lie on the bed but a nurse says, Now, now, no lying on the bed in the middle of the day. Your case isn't that serious' (p.260).

The improperly treated conjunctivitis is to trouble Frank for many years, compounded by his poor diet, poor hygiene and lack of medicine.

Q Explore the McCourt family's frustration when they fail to receive a telegram from England. How does McCourt set the reader up for this disappointment?

Q Using evidence from this chapter, explain whether you believe Angela is a good mother.

Chapter X (pp.269–90)

Summary: *Angela contracts pneumonia; Frank takes on responsibility for his mother and the children (pp.269–72); Guard Dennehy intervenes (pp.275–6); removal to Aunt Aggie's (p.277); Angela comes home from hospital (p.286); Malachy returns (p.285) and leaves again (pp.286–7); Frank sees his mother begging (p.288).*

Angela becomes desperately ill and Frank assumes the responsibility of caring for his mother and feeding his brothers. In her delirium, Angela begs for lemonade and Frank's solution is to steal both that and some food for the boys. It is a comment on the severity of their relatives that Frank would not think to ask for help from any of them. Frank's ability to provide is described in anecdotes strung together with wry comments, but the desperation behind the humour is evident (pp.269–72).

The reader is amused by Frank's verbal skills when he tries to prevent the Guards from discovering the state of the family (p.275). Nothing thwarts the march of authority, however, and the children are bundled off to stay with Aunt Aggie, but not before the poignancy of their situation is evoked when Grandma tells them to get their clothes and they can do nothing but stand there; they are wearing all they have (p.277).

The regime at Aunt Aggie's is harsh but relieved by the humorous anecdote of Aggie urinating into a chamber pot (p.278). Aggie is irritated by Frank, and nags at him all the time; Frank does not understand 'why she's always angry' (p.283) when she appears to live in relative luxury. Frank looks so like his father that Aggie is affronted by his presence:

> Aunt Aggie torments me all the time. She calls me scabby eyes. She says I'm the spitting image of my father, I have the odd manner, I have the sneaky air of a northern Presbyterian ... (p.284)

This episode in their lives is relieved by the kindness of Uncle Pa, who spoils them a little.

Frank thinks in his head Aggie is an 'Oul'bitch' (p.286), and is happy that his father suddenly appears and takes them home. Malachy stays only one day and is off again. Their hopes of a regular income are kindled when three pounds arrives the next Saturday, but 'the next Saturday there's no telegram nor the Saturday after nor any Saturday forever' (p.287).

In her despair, Angela sits by the fire 'puffing on her Woodbines', leaving the jam jars they use for glasses unwashed and 'flies in the sugar' (p.287) while Frank looks after his brothers – not always with the greatest care. Note the comedy of the anecdote of Alphie in the pram (pp.287–8) counterpointed against Frank's discovery of his mother begging from the priests' house:

> There in the middle of the crowd ... is my mother. This is my own mother, begging. This is worse than the dole, the St. Vincent de Paul Society, the Dispensary. It's the worst kind of shame ... and I push the pram up the street before she can see me. I don't want to go home anymore. (pp.288–9)

The meat she brings home, 'a little nipple of red meat' atop 'a great lump of quivering gray fat' (p.289), is given to Alphie the baby, who throws it to the dog.

Key point

This incident presages a change in Frank's relationship with his mother. He is ashamed of their utter destitution, a shame that will be magnified when they move later to Laman Griffin's place.

Q Explore McCourt's characterisation of his mother in this chapter. Is she presented as a sympathetic character? Support your answer with evidence from the text.

Chapter XI (pp.291–310)

Summary: *Frank discovers he was conceived before marriage (p.291); he ponders on the nature of doom (pp.293–5); he gets a job delivering coal (p.298); Frank loses his job (p.307).*

In searching for something to wear to play soccer, Frank finds his parents' marriage certificate, discovering that he was born in 'half the time' and therefore 'must be a miracle' (p.291). He decides to consult with Mikey Molloy, who is about to be initiated into 'the pint' (drinking Guinness at the pub) because he is now sixteen and no longer has fits. Mikey remains the expert in sexual matters, explaining the nature of conception and telling Frank: 'You're a bastard. You're doomed' (p.293). Frank is puzzled that he is not in a state of grace when it is not his fault that he was conceived out of wedlock.

Frank decides to light a penny candle to save himself 'from the doom' (p.295), but is swayed instead by the lure of toffee. He attempts to appease the Virgin Mary by promising that 'the next penny I get I'll be lighting a candle and would she please talk to her Son and delay the doom for awhile' (p.295). Frank kicks the winning goal in his soccer match and then believes that if he is really doomed, God would not have sent the ball right on to his foot.

Angela is persuaded to let the eleven-year-old Frank help Mr Hannon deliver coal to earn a little money. Frank is delighted at being initiated into 'real work', and becomes very fond of Mr Hannon who knows that Frank must become educated so that he can get out of Ireland and away from the poverty and the meanness of society there. Frank thinks he is now a 'man' and that he could leave school and deliver coal to provide for the family. It is the worst job he could do because his eyes are badly affected by the coal dust, and the conjunctivitis recurs. Nevertheless, he gains the respect of his schoolmates because he has learned to drive the horse and dray: 'they don't call me names anymore' (p.305). When he brings home five shillings he is baffled that Angela sits by the fire and cries. She realises that this is not fit work for Frank. He cries because he had envisioned bringing home 'the money the telegram boy never brought from my father' (p.307).

Q Why is it so important to Frank that he be able to work?

Chapter XII (pp.311–30)

Summary: *Malachy returns but he has not changed (pp.312–15); example of extreme poverty (pp.315–18); Angela's generosity (p.317); the radio and Shakespeare (pp.318–19); rent unpaid and walls burned for firewood (pp.320–2); Laman Griffin (pp.322–9).*

Malachy promises he is a 'new man' and is coming home. He returns drunk, bearing only half a box of chocolates and pretending to have no money – though he has enough to get drunk before he leaves again, this time forever (p.315). Frank compares their miserable existence with that of other boys on the Lanes (p.316).

Frank sits outside his grandmother's house listening to her neighbour's wireless radio where he hears all the great plays broadcast: 'Shakespeare is like mashed potatoes, you can never get enough of him' (pp.318–19). The neighbours, Mrs Purcell and her daughter Kathleen, are kind and ask him in to listen to *Macbeth*, feeding him bread and jam. He hears the music of Duke Ellington and Billie Holiday, and longs for a return to America.

'The rent man is losing his patience' because their payment is four weeks overdue (p.320). The family fails to raise the rent money, and when the landlord comes to investigate, he discovers that they have torn down the wall dividing the flat's two rooms and used it for firewood. They are evicted, and Grandma arranges for them to go to stay with Angela's cousin, Laman Griffin. Frank regrets the loss of the 'Angel on the Seventh Step' but feels he is now too grown up, at twelve, for angels (p.324).

Life at Laman's promises to be better; at least there is a lavatory, and Malachy sees back gardens where 'they're growing things ... We can have our own spuds and everything' (p.325). Laman, however, proves to be a lazy, mean man who treats both Angela and Frank like servants. He is too indolent to go to the library and sends Frank instead. This gives Frank the opportunity to read whatever he wishes.

In a short aside, Frank relates that the sour-faced grandmother catches pneumonia and dies, unmourned.

Chapter XIII (pp.331–45)

Summary: *Laman promises Frank his bicycle but brutalises him instead (pp.331–2, 342–3); Frank attempts to continue his education through the Christian Brothers, but the Church fails him (p.337); Frank becomes obsessed with sex (pp.340–2); Laman beats Frank and he runs away (pp.343–5).*

Laman is an exploiter and promises Frank the use of his bicycle if he empties his chamber pot every morning. Frank agrees but vomits; Angela feels Frank's humiliation and 'stares into the dead ashes' (p.332).

At the library, Frank reads *Butler's Lives of the Saints* and discovers 'they're worse than any horror film' (p.333). His investigation of the meaning of 'virgin' is comic, all the more so because the librarian believes he is pious. His headmaster also believes he has 'a mind for the priesthood' (p.336) and sends him with his mother to the Christian Brothers in the hope of further education. 'We don't have room for him, says Brother Murray and closes the door in our faces' (p.337). Angela reminds him, 'that's the second time a door was slammed in your face by the Church' and 'she starts to cry by the fire' (p.338). Frank just wants a job at this stage because he is thirteen and in his last year at school.

Frank becomes aware that Angela is having sex with Laman and he is disgusted and confused, for the Church has buried any references to sexual matters in euphemism. Such fear has been invoked about the consequences of masturbation that Frank believes he is damned. Again the scene of his Confession is amusing, as the priest, who asks Frank whether his dirty acts have been committed on his own, with someone else or 'with some class of beast', opens up 'new worlds' to Frank (p.342).

Failure to empty the chamber pot becomes the catalyst for Frank to be beaten by the beastly Laman. Frank is ready to kill Laman when his mother has sex with him again to appease him (pp.343–4). Frank leaves in pain and utter disgust, ending up at his Uncle Pat's where, in the absence of food, he takes 'the greasy newspaper from the floor' and licks and sucks 'the paper till there isn't a smidgen of grease' (p.345). This is a major turning point for Frank, leaving his family for an unknown future.

Chapter XIV (pp.346–60)

Summary: *Frank dreams of how life will be when he is working (pp.346–7); Frank's shame over their poverty (p.347), shame over his appearance, and humiliation over wearing Grandma's dress (pp.358–60).*

Frank resists pleas from Michael to return to Laman's but mentally promises to 'buy proper clothes for the whole family' (p.347) when he starts his job. Uncle Pat refuses to provide Frank with food and so he steals, believing that the Church ranks masturbation as far worse a sin than theft (p.349). He scrounges food and still delights in reading about the saints now that he has his own library card. While inadvertently reading a book of Chinese essays on love he discovers that his father lied to him for years about 'the Angel on the Seventh Step'; the librarian, yet another custodian of authority, banishes him for reading 'filth' (p.355).

The day before his fourteenth birthday he sees himself in Grandma's mirror as he really is: 'my eyes are red and oozing yellow' (p.356), he has pimples and black, rotten teeth. Worst of all, though, he has no shoulders, and wonders if the power of prayer could induce them to widen (p.357). He is about to start work as a telegram boy and realises his clothes are a disgrace. He takes them off to wash them, resulting in one of the funniest anecdotes in the book. It is cold and damp and the only thing to wear is an old black dress left by his grandmother, so he goes to bed thinking that he will never be seen. Unfortunately Uncle Pat has a fall and Aunt Aggie comes and finds him; the neighbours see him, and Frank is mortified at the scandal that will ensue: 'you might as well stick your head out the window and make a general announcement about yourself and the dress problem' (p.360).

Chapter XV (pp.361–81)

Summary: *Aunt Aggie buys Frank clothes (p.363); he begins work as a telegram boy (p.363); starts saving to return to America (p.367); has his first sexual experience (p.379); mourns Theresa Carmody (pp.380–1).*

Aunt Aggie is impressed by Frank's desire to make a better future for his family, and realises he is not like his father at all. She reveals a hidden kindness by buying him new clothes for his first day at work (p.363), a kindness that moves him to tears. Later he suspects she went into debt to do so.

In this chapter McCourt's anecdotal style is at its best as he weaves stories around the people he encounters on his telegram rounds. Frank meets up with old friends, updating the reader's knowledge of what has happened to earlier characters, like the Clohessys, whose standard of living has improved dramatically with Paddy and his father working in England (pp.364–5).

The first real wages are sweet and Frank squanders nearly all of the money before realising that he must begin saving immediately if he is to reach America by the time he is twenty. Sometimes he is lucky and receives tips and, in concert with the rest of his experiences, he finds that the poor tip and the rich do not.

Frank's innate kindness is highlighted in this chapter when, despite instructions to the contrary, he performs small tasks for some of the helpless people he meets such as 'the pile of rags' and 'the old man from the Boer War' (p.370). He contrasts their plight with the wealth of the Prime Minister, de Valera, and that of the priests and nuns who are always telling their parishioners that it is no shame to be poor while lorries drive 'up to their houses with crates and barrels of whiskey and wine' (p.371).

Such hypocrisy is anathema to Frank, who now rides down streets that are worse than any of the Lanes the family has inhabited.

Now that Frank is earning money, Angela and the boys move in to Uncle Pat's; Frank has to support them, but at least they are all together again, telling stories and dreaming of America. Life is better now and Frank enjoys delivering to the country where he dawdles and delights in his freedom (p.377).

Frank meets Theresa Carmody in his weekly delivery to her family and this leads to his first sexual experience (p.379). He is distraught when Theresa, who has tuberculosis, dies; he believes he is responsible for sending her soul to hell, not knowing why he has 'a pain like this in my heart' (p.381). It is Frank's first adult experience of grief over the loss of a loved one.

Q Do you think Aunt Aggie redeems herself in the eyes of the reader in this chapter? Why or why not?

Q How does Frank's Catholic upbringing and understanding of 'sin' inform his grief over Theresa Carmody's death?

Chapter XVI (pp.382–96)

Summary: *Frank meets mad Mr Harrington (pp.382–4); is troubled by Theresa's death (p.386); encounters Mrs Finucane, a debt collector (pp.387–90); finds another job (pp.393–4).*

During the course of making his deliveries, Frank meets Mr Harrington, a Presbyterian, who is grieving for his wife. He is deranged and, after much comic interaction, causes Frank to momentarily lose his job (pp.382–6). Unable to go to Confession because he is tormented by the vision of Theresa's soul in hell, Frank decides to delay until he reaches America (pp.386–7).

Another cameo presented to the reader is Mrs Finucane, the moneylender. She employs Frank to write letters of demand to customers who have failed to pay back their loans. It is good training for him, but he becomes more and more outlandish in his vocabulary and scares such ordinary people as Angela's friends. Nevertheless, Mrs Finucane pays well and because she is mean and only using the money to buy Masses to be said for the repose of her soul, Frank has no qualms in stealing a few extra shillings when the chance arises (p.390). He has become ruthless in his quest to save money for America: 'if my whole family dropped from the hunger I wouldn't touch this money in the post office' (p.390).

On the day Frank is to take the exam for a permanent position as a telegram boy, which would secure for him a safe pension, he applies instead to an advertisement for a 'smart boy'. Encouraged by Uncle Pa Keating to go ahead and not be tied down to life in Limerick, he is given a job as a newspaper distributor (pp.393–4). He is humiliated by Mrs O'Connell and Miss Barry at the post office when he returns his belt and pouch, because he is working 'for that pack of freemasons and Protestants above in Dublin' (p.396). Frank, however, doesn't know what he did wrong.

Chapter XVII (pp.397–415)

Summary: *Uncle Pa stands Frank his first pint (p.398); he hits his mother (p.400); he seeks reassurance from St. Francis (pp.402–3); censorship (pp.408–11).*

Frank gets drunk when Uncle Pa stands (buys) him his first pint, and from the men in the pub he discovers that World War II has ended. This has little impact on Frank's life or on the pace of life in Limerick, except by giving some of the men a chance to work for better money in England.

In his inebriated state, Frank tries to confess the sins that have been accumulating since Theresa's death but, again, the minions of the Church slam the door in his face and refuse to help (p.399).

At home Angela is 'by the fire smoking a Woodbine' (p.399). She accuses Frank of being 'just like your father' and, stung, Frank says he would rather be like his father than like Laman Griffin (p.400). 'She turns away … and looks into the ashes' (p.400). He is insolent, unable, directly, to explain his hurt and disgust at her relationship with Laman. He is still only sixteen and, with the innocence of youth, cannot understand either her physical or emotional needs. After all, Angela herself is still only in her mid-thirties. He hits her and, although he regrets hurting her, he is still unable to forgive her (pp.400–1).

In his despair, Frank seeks solace at the Franciscan Church and accuses St. Francis of refusing to help him. It is his sixteenth birthday and he is miserable but then 'there is an arm around my shoulders, a brown robe, click of black rosary beads, a Franciscan priest' (p.402). This is a moving scene where Frank is, at last, able to empty from his mind the store of pent-up emotions that have troubled him for years. He is reassured and he is 'happy' (p.403).

Frank's new job is a challenge but also offers opportunity. For example, the intensely Catholic Mr McCaffrey tries to remove all page sixteens from a Presbyterian magazine because they contain material on birth control, going from shop to shop ripping the magazine apart, making it impossible for the shopkeepers to sell it (p.410). Frank, inspired by his colleague Eamon's idea, turns this incident to his own advantage, collecting most of the rejected pages and selling them at an exorbitant price, not at all concerned that the customers 'are in danger of losing their immortal souls' (p.410). That entrepreneurial act contributes eight pounds to his savings account.

Q How is the reader positioned to view Frank's drunken behaviour in this chapter?

Chapter XVIII (pp.416–25)

Summary: *Mrs Finucane dies (p.416); Frank has enough money for his fare (p.417); Angela gives a party and Frank sails (pp.418–20).*

The tale is progressed rapidly: 'I'm seventeen, eighteen, going on nineteen' (p.416) and Frank has built up his bank account. When Mrs Finucane conveniently dies, Frank helps himself to her cash and the ledger of debtors. When Frank finds Aunt Aggie's name in the ledger, he assumes, as does the reader, that she went into that debt to pay for Frank's new clothes. The reader rejoices when Frank decides to 'heave the ledger into the river' (p.417), as all the bad debts of the poor go with it.

With the money taken from Mrs Finucane, Frank is finally able to set in motion his plans to return to America. Now Frank must imprint scenes of Limerick in his mind, for he may never return. The immigrant must always face this crisis, because no matter how bad the conditions in the home country are, it is just that, home. The future is uncertain and fraught with unknown dangers but ''Tis the beginning for Frankie McCourt', and he sails on the *Irish Oak* for America (p.420).

Q How is the reader invited to respond to Frank's actions towards Mrs Finucane? Is Frank's portrait of her as a mean, selfish woman who preys on the poor reliable? Is Frank justified in taking the money?

Chapter XIX (p.426)

The single word chapter, ''Tis' (with no closing punctuation), seems to leave us abruptly in the middle of the story. But in fact it is the end of Frank's youth, the end of his life in Ireland with all its suffering and hardship, and the beginning of a new life in America. As an ending to a tale of incredible suffering and hardship it promises the beginnings of a very new and different future. *Angela's Ashes* thus ends on a strongly affirmative note, responding to the Wireless Officer's query aboard the ship about the greatness of America (p.425). *'Tis* is also the title of McCourt's follow-up memoir, released in 1999.

CHARACTERS & RELATIONSHIPS

Frank McCourt

As a memoir, the whole of the action revolves around Frank's narration. It is through his eyes that the reader follows the interaction of characters, all of whom relate to him in some way. The reader is taken on a journey from before Frank's conception to his return to America; for him, it is a journey from innocence to maturity, and the reader is allowed to participate in that journey – but only from Frank's point of view.

Frank's development

It is important to identify and reflect upon the key experiences that mark Frank's development. The following are examples of ways you might identify, describe and analyse Frank's development.

1 Presenting events in chronological order provides an accessible entry to the wealth of detail and is a logical way to highlight first experiences and how they change Frank's outlook and behaviour.

2 Exploration of Frank's emotional, intellectual and moral/spiritual growth provides another organising principle that will facilitate intelligent analysis and depth of understanding. For example, emotional development will encompass lack of love from his mother and family; a recurring sense of shame regarding his own inadequacies and his family's destitution; his need for sexual love; and his increasing self-confidence and self-esteem. Intellectual development covers his ability to learn and the growth of his imagination, helped along by his father. Frank's schooling likewise plays a crucial role in this regard; his experiences at school are not always positive but Mr O'Halloran opens up his mind to the power of learning, as does Mr Timoney. Even Laman plays a role, giving him access to the library. Important milestones for Frank

include his discovery of Shakespeare and of poetry (in learning 'The Highwayman'). Frank's moral development is linked with the Church. Its teachings are undermined by the double standards he experiences (see 'Brief overview of Frank' section below).

3 Relationships with family members and significant friends and acquaintances also provide valuable insights into Frank's growth. Consider the positive and negative impact of these individuals on his development.

Activity Select three or four of the following key scenes or events and write a paragraph explaining their significance.

- Frank commences school (p.83)
- Frank's First Communion (Chapter IV)
- Frank's First Confession (p.140)
- Frank's rejection by the Church: as an altar boy (p.167); as a student with the Christian Brothers (p.337); for wanting to make a Confession when drunk (p.399)
- Frank meets Mr Timoney (pp.196–202)
- Frank's time in the hospital, first with typhoid fever (pp.216–30) then with severe conjunctivitis (pp.259–64)
- Frank meets Mr O'Halloran, an inspirational teacher (pp.235–7)
- Frank sees his mother begging (p.288)
- Frank runs away after Laman Griffin breaks his promise to lend him his bike and instead beats him (pp.342–5)
- Frank's first 'real' job – telegram boy (p.363)
- Frank's first pint (pp.398–400)

Can you think of any other events in Frank's life that are crucial to his development? List them.

Brief overview of Frank

Frank is an engaging character and as the reader follows his development he is seen with all his strengths and weaknesses. Perhaps his greatest strength is his innate humanity, his instinctive knowledge of what is 'right' and what is 'wrong'. Thus, the ill treatment of Frank at the hands of practitioners of the Catholic faith works to highlight the apparent hypocrisy of the Church. Frank suffers and the reader feels this suffering acutely. When Frank steals or lies, however, the reader is asked to accept this behaviour and excuse him. Nevertheless, when he hits his mother because of his teenage intolerance, the reader is encouraged to feel sympathy for Angela, who is witnessing her son display the same aberrant behaviour as his father before him. Indeed, the adult narrator does not ask the reader to excuse this conduct; it is one of the rare moments when Frank does something unambiguously wrong.

The reader is invited to decide if there is anything special about Frank. He is portrayed as 'ordinary', the son of an incurable alcoholic father and a hopeless mother. Worse than working class, he belongs to the inveterate poor, those unable to help themselves, and yet the reader does not feel that Frank is helpless. Even before he goes to work, events suggest that he is not, as Aunt Aggie believes, like his father. He wants to escape the poverty into which he was born. He has a steely streak of determination that sets him above the rest of his family and above the rest of the children in the neighbourhood.

It is entirely consistent with his character that he does not take the exam for the 'safe' job as telegram boy, leading to a comfortable pension; that he instead breaks the cycle and strikes out for a better life in America. Thus, the reader is likely to accept that Frank steals Mrs Finucane's money not because Mrs Finucane has no-one to leave the money to, but because it is consistent with Frank's ruthlessness in his quest to save the fare for America and his determination to use any means possible to do so.

Frank is not humble, either. He is a proud boy who is confused by many aspects of his own life, particularly as to why there are no explanations given about such ordinary matters as human sexuality. He is puzzled by the meanness of others, of those who are better off than his family and, more particularly, of those relatives who seem to have more than enough to spare but who never show any generosity or kindness towards himself or his family.

Malachy McCourt

Frank's father is proud, but it is an unjustified pride. He refuses to ask for help; for example, when he is working as a farmhand, he would rather see his family starve than ask to take some vegetables home for them. On the other hand, he is ready to beg for 'a pint' at any time. He schools his son in the kind of pride Frank must cultivate: he must 'never carry things'; he must always wear 'a collar and tie' (pp.101–2). He takes pride in his position as a male and believes that these things contribute to his masculine identity.

He is, nevertheless, a hopeless alcoholic, unable to provide even the most basic necessities of food and shelter for his ever-increasing family. Even when he works, he spends all the money on Guinness and comes home drunk in the middle of the night singing patriotic songs of Ireland, imposing a warped idea of Irish history on Frank.

Malachy, though, is not an abuser. He loves his children and wants a better life for them, ensuring that they are literate at least. Above all, he is a storyteller and creates an imaginative world for Frank that is his alone. This is the priceless legacy that Malachy leaves Frank.

Angela McCourt

Frank's mother is characterised in the first chapter as 'useless'. She is worn down by poverty and endless pregnancies and, like her husband, she is unable to provide for the children because there is never enough money. The points of her humiliation are marked by the presence of ashes (which are both literal and symbolic), a motif that recurs throughout the story.

Frank's relationship with his mother is not as close as the one he has with his father, despite Malachy's inadequacies. Angela gives life to Frank and ensures his survival. In his mind, however, his father has given much more. Malachy helps to cultivate Frank's imagination, which helps Frank to remain mentally and emotionally strong. Angela takes care of the practical aspects of his life, although she often leaves him to take responsibility not just for himself but for his younger brothers as well.

It must be remembered, though, that Angela's mother has never had any affection for her and that her husband is the kind of male chauvinist who demands that she 'do her duty', although he has no intention of ever doing his. The text presents her as a victim of her upbringing, of her religion and of her society. She does not have Frank's capacity for rising above what fate has provided for her.

Grandma

The text depicts a number of Frank's relatives, from the MacNamara sisters of the first chapter to Frank's 'sour-eyed' grandmother. Her only contribution to Frank's upbringing is to mete out strictures and make sure he is raised as a pious young Irish Catholic. She ensures that Frank has all the special trappings for his first Holy Communion but she is furious when Frank throws up his celebratory breakfast, and insists that he make his Confession again. The priest's barely stifled mirth changes to impatience when Grandma makes Frank return yet again to see if she should wash away God with ordinary or holy water. This is the measure of her Catholicism. There are times when she refuses to speak to the family – and these times are 'bad … because we can't run to her when we need to borrow sugar or tea or milk' (p.147). Importantly, it is only in a negative context that we learn of any help at all from Grandma. Further, it is a mark of her lack of significance in Frank's life that her death is noted only as an afterthought at the end of a chapter. She, too, is poor but she has a regular income, which she is loath to share with Angela's indigent family. In the first chapter, she characterises Angela as 'useless' and sends her off to America to get rid of her, showing how little her own pious devotion to the Church has to do with Christian charity.

Aunt Aggie

One of the cruellest relatives is Aunt Aggie, who picks on Frank for two reasons. Firstly, she resents Angela's fertility when she, herself, is barren. Although she appears to Frank to have all the comforts for a reasonable existence, her inability to have a family of her own leaves her dissatisfied and bad-tempered. Secondly, Frank closely resembles his father in appearance. He is, therefore, an affront to Aunt Aggie who thinks that because Frank looks like his father, he will also become a feckless alcoholic like Malachy. However, when she realises that Frank is eager to work and support his mother and brothers, she buys him decent clothes for his first job (possibly going into debt to do so), redeeming herself to some extent.

Aunt Aggie's meanness is somewhat relieved by her husband, the generous Uncle Pa Keating, who appears in the story intermittently. It is he who treats Frank to his first 'pint', an initiation usually reserved for the father.

Laman Griffin

When the family are evicted from Roden Lane they seek shelter with Angela's cousin. Laman is mean, lazy and brutish, with no redeeming qualities. Inadvertently, he gives Frank access to the library because he is too lazy to go himself (pp.328–9). He takes in the McCourts only to exploit them, so Frank ends up emptying his chamber pot while Angela appeases him with sex. When he breaks his promise of the loan of his bike to Frank, he cannot stand Frank's repeated refrain, 'You promised me'; he beats Frank in a fury, threatening to kill the 'little shit' (p.343). Frank runs away. This incident demonstrates both the greater refusal of Frank to be so unjustly treated and the level to which the helpless Angela has sunk, for which Frank cannot forgive her.

Mr O'Halloran

Mr O'Halloran, Frank's teacher in sixth class and the headmaster, has a lasting impact on him. He makes the boys learn everything by heart. 'He loves America and makes us know all the American states in alphabetical order' (p.235). He gives them a thorough grounding in Irish grammar and history, but more significantly he teaches them 'what is important and why' (p.236). He confronts Frank with the fact that the Irish committed atrocities just as the English did and, impossible as this idea seems to him, Frank accepts that it must be true because Mr O'Halloran is the headmaster. He leaves Frank an enduring legacy – the value of a well-stocked mind: 'you might be poor ... but your mind is a palace' (p.237).

However, Mr O'Halloran's attempts to rectify the injustice of poverty and provide 'strong warm boots for the winter' (p.237) elude Frank when he and Malachy miss out (after running all over Limerick selling raffle tickets) and eleven boys without boots get them instead.

Miscellaneous characters

There are many characters, some Frank's peers, who contribute to the advancement of the story. Most of them are placed within self-contained anecdotes but many, like Mikey Molloy and Paddy Clohessy, are woven intermittently through the narrative. These lesser characters provide much of the substance for the tale, as well as helping to demonstrate Frank's advancement from innocence to maturity. It is through them that the author shows the kindness of ordinary people in contrast to the meanness of Frank's relatives and authority figures. Even a minor character like Patricia Madigan takes on a greater significance because she assists Frank's imaginative development. These cameo appearances are also used to underline the main themes and support McCourt's account of the social conditions in Limerick in the 1930s and 40s.

Activity Make brief notes on each of the following characters and their importance.

- Mikey Molloy (pp.124–9; p.211; pp.292–5)
- Brendan ('Question') Quigley (pp.130–2)
- The Clohessys (pp.132–3; pp.184–90; pp.364–6); Paddy (pp.169–72)
- Mr Timoney (pp.196–202; pp.261–2)
- Patricia Madigan (pp.218–25)
- Mr Hannon (pp.297–310)
- Mrs Purcell and Kathleen (pp.318–20)
- Theresa Carmody (pp.378–81; p.386; pp.402–3)

THEMES, IDEAS & VALUES

Growing up

Frank's development from an innocent child of three to a mature nineteen-year-old is the predominant theme of this memoir. Every part of Frank's development is consistent with the age specified by the author and should be looked at as a path to self-awareness, rather than as achievement. The text suggests that it will be in America that Frank really finds himself. Life in Limerick is merely a preliminary, yet the young Frank's experiences also determine the kind of man he will be. In many ways the memoir has become a celebration of the young man's survival.

Immigration

Frank's character is partly formed by his status as an immigrant. Throughout the book it is his aim to return to the land of his birth. Because he was only four when the family moved to Ireland, he is possessed by the knowledge that a different future was once possible for him. A return to America symbolises a return to a sane life, an opportunity to cast off the endemic poverty of Limerick. All the characters who care about Frank – his father, Uncle Pat, Mr Hannon, his headmaster (Mr O'Halloran) and Mr Timoney – urge Frank to move out of Limerick. They are aware that Frank's future will be similar to that of all the Lane folk if he remains in Ireland. With his demonstrated intelligence, it is important that Frank escape the limiting social conditions of Limerick to attain a better standard of living in America.

Authority

Frank encounters the harshness of authority at every stage of his development. Except for his parents and other poor Lane families, the adults all seem to pursue a regime of harshness well beyond that normally apparent to a child. While one expects the school system of that era to have been strict, its inflexibility and limitations ensure that fear is the only means of controlling the boys. Fortunately that fails in most instances, for Frank and his peers are rarely cowed.

The Church has little regard for the poor in its flock. It is only at the level of the parish priest that Frank encounters any sympathy or humanity from the Church, which is so ready to shut the door in Frank's face. This sense of rejection by the Church marks several stages of Frank's development.

The authority of his relatives, with their coldness and austerity, perhaps damages Frank most of all. It is only within the confines of the immediate family that there is comfort. Outside of it, the relatives just do not care. It is only their sense of duty that is called on at crucial points of development in the story, not their kindness. The McCourts are unwanted and unloved, merely a nuisance.

Family

Frank is always happy when the family is together, despite the endemic poverty. Even when he is three years old, Frank is shown to have a mutually loving relationship with his brother. Frank accepts, without question, the expansion of the family and even though it becomes increasingly dysfunctional, there is always warmth and comfort and loving kindness. The family members are mutually cooperative in their attempts to survive. None of the siblings ever question the need to participate fully in providing what little can be found in the way of shelter, warmth and, above all, food. It is this quest for survival that melds the siblings in particular into a unit that can withstand the humiliations inflicted upon them by the authority of the relatives, of the Church and of charity.

Poverty, alcoholism and survival

The destitute situation of the family and Malachy's alcoholism are the predominant limitations affecting Frank's life. He learns to accept his father's unemployment, but never the drunkenness. Gradually Frank perceives that there are other ways to live and that it is because of his father's alcoholism that they are starving. Frank cannot understand this kind of dereliction of duty and, finally, stops accepting it. After that, Malachy becomes a shadowy figure in the story – but Frank's adult character has already been determined by the damage inflicted upon him as a child. The quest for food governs their lives and the lives of all the poor families in Limerick. There is never enough food and Frank learns to steal and cajole, even to beg, suffering the attendant shame. He endures a humiliation that the author portrays with the depth of feeling that only comes from experience. It is, however, the laughter and the joy that Frank delights in that remain with the reader. The bitterness of the family's poverty and the fight for mere survival are never allowed to triumph over the innocent delight of the maturing child.

QUESTIONS & ANSWERS

This section focuses on your own analytical writing on the text, and gives you strategies for producing high-quality responses in your coursework and exam essays.

Essay writing – an overview

An essay on a literary work is a formal and serious piece of writing that presents your point of view on the text, usually in response to a given topic. Your 'point of view' in an essay is your interpretation of the meaning of the text's language, structure, characters, situations and events, supported by detailed analysis of textual evidence.

Analyse – don't summarise

In your essays it is important to avoid simply summarising what happens in a text.

- A **summary** is a description or paraphrase (retelling in different words) of the characters and events. For example: 'Macbeth has a horrifying vision of a dagger dripping with blood before he goes to murder King Duncan.'
- An **analysis** is an explanation of the real meaning or significance that lies 'beneath' the text's words (and images, for a film). For example: 'Macbeth's vision of a bloody dagger shows how deeply uneasy he is about the violent act he is contemplating, and conveys his sense that supernatural forces are impelling him to act.'

A limited amount of summary is sometimes necessary to let your reader know which part of the text you wish to discuss. However, always keep this to a minimum and follow it immediately with your analysis of what this part of the text is really telling us.

Plan your essay

Carefully plan your essay so that you have a clear idea of what you are going to say. The plan ensures that your ideas flow logically, that your argument remains consistent and that you stay on the topic. An essay plan should be a list of **brief dot points** covering no more than half a page.

- Include your central argument or main contention – a concise statement of your overall response to the topic.
- Write three or four dot points for each paragraph, indicating the main idea and evidence/examples from the text. Note that in your essay you will need to *expand* on these points and *analyse* the evidence.

Structure your essay

An essay is a complete, self-contained piece of writing. It has a clear beginning (the introduction), middle (several body paragraphs) and end (the last paragraph or conclusion). It must also have a central argument that runs throughout, linking each paragraph to form a coherent whole. See examples of introductions and conclusions in the 'Analysing a sample topic' and 'Sample answer' sections.

The introduction establishes your overall response to the topic. It includes your main contention and outlines the main evidence you will refer to in the course of the essay. Write your introduction *after* you have done a plan and *before* you write the rest of the essay.

The body paragraphs argue your case – they present evidence from the text and explain how this evidence supports your argument. Each body paragraph needs:

- a strong **topic sentence** (usually the first sentence) that states the main point being made in the paragraph
- **evidence** from the text, including some brief quotations
- **analysis** of the textual evidence, with **explanation** of its significance and how it supports your argument
- **links back to the topic** in one or more statements, usually towards the end of the paragraph.

Connect the body paragraphs so that your discussion flows smoothly. Use some linking words and phrases such as 'similarly' and 'on the other hand', though don't start every paragraph like this. Another strategy is to use a significant word from the last sentence of one paragraph in the first sentence of the next.

Use key terms from the topic – or synonyms for them – throughout, so the relevance of your discussion to the topic is always clear.

The conclusion ties everything together and finishes the essay. It includes strong statements that emphasise your central argument and provide a clear response to the topic.

Avoid simply restating the points made earlier in the essay – this will end on a very flat note and imply that you have run out of ideas and vocabulary. The conclusion should be a logical extension of what you have written, not just a repetition or summary of it. Writing an effective conclusion can be a challenge. Try using these tips:

- Start by linking back to the final sentence of the second-last paragraph – this helps your writing to flow, rather than leaping back to your main contention straight away.
- Use synonyms and expressions with equivalent meanings to vary your vocabulary. This allows you to reinforce your line of argument without being repetitive.
- When planning your essay, think of one or two broad statements or observations about the text's wider meaning. These should be related to the topic and your overall argument. Keep them for the conclusion, since they will give you something 'new' to say but still follow logically from your discussion. The introduction will be focused on the topic, but the conclusion can present a wider view of the text.

Essay topics

1. "Day and night I dream of America." How does Frank overcome the odds against him and make his dream come true?
2. 'Drinking is depicted as a rite of passage in *Angela's Ashes.*' Explore the role of alcohol and alcoholism in the text.
3. 'The relatives from both sides of Frank's family are cruel and miserly.' To what extent do you agree?
4. 'In *Angela's Ashes*, the poor are shown to be kind and generous where the privileged are mean and harsh.' Do you agree?
5. "It's like having jewels in my mouth when I say the words." What role does language and storytelling play in Frank's life?
6. How and why do Frank's feelings towards his father change as he grows up?
7. 'Frank's relationship with his mother is complex and undermined by poverty.' Discuss.
8. 'The Church slams the door in Frank's face three times, yet it also provides guidance and support.' To what extent do you agree?
9. What is the effect of the anecdotes woven throughout *Angela's Ashes*?
10. 'It is the combination of the humorous and the absurd that relieves the bleakness of the text.' Discuss.

Analysing a sample topic

'In *Angela's Ashes*, the poor are shown to be kind and generous where the privileged are mean and harsh.' Do you agree?

Identify the key terms in the question in order to unpack the definitions and synonyms.

'In *Angela's Ashes*, **the poor** are shown to be **kind** and **generous** where **the privileged** are **mean** and **harsh**.'

- The poor: the underprivileged, poverty-stricken or destitute (i.e. the other residents of the Limerick Lanes, or those who, like Angela, beg at the St. Vincent de Paul Society).
- Kind: caring, sympathetic, humane.
- Generous: giving, charitable, open-handed.
- The privileged: the rich, the fortunate, those in a position of authority.
- Mean: cruel, callous, malicious.
- Harsh: strict, severe, insensitive, punitive.

The preamble to the prompt ('In *Angela's Ashes*') indicates that you will need to provide examples from throughout the text. Be sure not to focus on only one particular section or character.

Which characters can you identify as being poor as well as kind and generous? Can you think of any who are poor while also being rude or stingy? Who are the privileged characters in *Angela's Ashes*? Are they mean and harsh, or caring and charitable?

You need to make your contention clear in the introduction and indicate your line of argument. The following plan is one way to tackle the topic. While the weight of the evidence in the text supports the topic statement, you could also provide a more qualified answer.

Sample introduction

> Frank McCourt's memoir *Angela's Ashes* paints a stark but surprisingly uplifting picture of life in the poverty-stricken Lanes of 1930s Limerick. Frank and his family encounter destitution, hunger, horrific living conditions and disease; they are forced to beg, borrow and steal just to survive. During these trying times, the McCourts often find support in unlikely places, offered by those who have little more than them and are in no real position to provide charity. In contrast, in Limerick especially, when the McCourts look to the Church and even to the members of their own extended family who are well-off by comparison, they experience rejection and

judgement. While there are some notable exceptions, more often than not, in *Angela's Ashes*, it is the less fortunate who show generosity and kindness, while those in a position of privilege turn a blind eye.

Body paragraph outline

Paragraph 1: The poorest are often those who show the most kindness and generosity in *Angela's Ashes*.

- When baby Margaret dies, Angela and Malachy fall into depression and neglect their remaining children. Their neighbours in the Brooklyn tenement, Mrs Leibowitz and Minnie MacAdorey, who have more money than the McCourts but would still be classified as poor, ensure the children are fed and taken care of.
- As a telegram boy, Frank reveals that the rich (or more often their servants) fail to tip, where 'widows, Protestant ministers' wives and the poor in general' (p.368) always do.
- Frank risks his position as a telegram boy in order to cash money orders for the residents of the Lanes who are 'helpless to get out of the bed to go to the post office' (p.370). These are the poorest of the poor, and even they offer him a 'little tip' and will not let Frank refuse it (p.372).
- Angela cannot bring herself to turn away beggars she encounters in the street, inviting them home for tea and bread. Despite relying on money from the St. Vincent de Paul Society to feed herself and her boys, 'she says there are always people worse off and we can surely spare a little from what we have' (p.317).

Paragraph 2: In Limerick, the most privileged in society (the Church, in particular) are often shown to be the most close-fisted.

- Representatives of the Church in the 1930s would have been highly regarded and would not have gone hungry as their parishioners did, but the text shows the Catholic Church to be uncaring with regard to the plight of the poor.

- The Church preaches the nobility of poverty, while 'lorries [drive] up to their houses with crates and barrels of whiskey and wine, eggs galore and legs of ham' (p.371).
- The men at the Dispensary mete out charity only after having thoroughly humiliated the poor families seeking assistance, including the McCourts (pp.266–8).

Paragraph 3: While, more often than not, the poor are shown to be kinder and more generous than the rich in *Angela's Ashes*, there are some notable exceptions.

- In the memoir's early chapters, the Italian grocers, who are considerably more privileged than the destitute McCourts, go out of their way to help Angela and her sons. They allow Angela an advance on her groceries (p.21) and when Frank steals a bunch of bananas to feed himself and his hungry brothers, rather than punishing him, they give him a bag of fruit to take home (p.27).
- While members of the McCourts' own extended family, who are well-off in comparison, offer assistance begrudgingly, they do help when they can. Though she constantly berates the boys, and Frank in particular, Aunt Aggie does take them in when Angela contracts pneumonia, and she buys Frank a new suit to wear on his telegram rounds (it is later suggested that this puts her in debt).
- Though many representatives of the Church fail to live up to the Christian values of compassion and charity, one notable exception is the Dominican priest, to whom Frank confesses that, out of hunger, he has stolen fish and chips. In response, the priest tells him, 'My child, I sit here. I hear the sins of the poor. I assign the penance. I bestow absolution. I should be on my knees washing their feet' (p.209).

Sample conclusion

Dealing as it does with the consequences of alcoholism and extreme poverty, *Angela's Ashes* is at times a disturbing read. However, the misery of life in the Lanes of Limerick is undercut by the many anecdotes that highlight the humanity of ordinary people who are willing to share what little they have with those less fortunate. Throughout his memoir, McCourt condemns the Catholic Church's neglect of the poor during this period, although he does include examples of Church representatives who are sensitive to the plight of the poor. More often, however, he celebrates a sense of shared experience among the poverty-stricken, who look out for one another despite their trying circumstances.

SAMPLE ANSWER

What is the effect of the anecdotes woven throughout *Angela's Ashes*?

The form of *Angela's Ashes* – a memoir comprised of a series of anecdotes – reflects the tradition of Irish storytelling referenced throughout the narrative. To some extent, *Angela's Ashes* as a whole could be thought of as a collection of anecdotes, loosely strung together to form the narrative of Frank's childhood and adolescence in the poverty-stricken Lanes of Limerick in the 1930s. These self-contained, wryly humorous stories advance the main narrative of Frank's life, and thus function collectively as a structuring device. Anecdotes also aid in the characterisation of Frank, his family and the supporting characters in the Lanes, and help to engage the reader emotionally with these characters and the trials they face.

In *Angela's Ashes*, the chapter divisions are the primary structuring feature, allowing certain events to be contained in one section at a time, with transitional features to join the chapters together. For example, Chapter I contains all the material from America, with the family leaving for Ireland at the chapter's close. Thus, a transition is made in the text while the family travels between countries: at the start of Chapter II the family arrives in Ireland and a new era begins. It is an effective way of progressing the narrative without a detailed description of the journey. The use of anecdote functions similarly as a structural device, one that is utilised *within* each chapter, progressing the narrative through loosely linked self-contained recollections.

McCourt takes this device further by supplementing his own memories with the stories of other people living in Limerick at the time, such as Mikey Molloy. While these anecdotes do not necessarily revolve around main characters, they do serve to advance Frank's development. In Mikey's case, he is the custodian of Frank's sexual development and appears at strategic moments in the tale. Furthermore, the shorter, seemingly less noteworthy anecdotes of people such as 'the pile of rags' and 'the man from the Boer War' serve a dual purpose, illustrating Frank's innate humanity while also adding depth to the social history McCourt is creating.

It is the anecdotes involving the McCourt family directly, however, that form the main narrative thread of *Angela's Ashes*, and it is through these stories that we get a sense of the social setting of the Limerick Lanes and each character's way of dealing with the circumstances in which they find themselves. Incidents such as the attempt to hang the Pope's picture in Roden Lane, for example, highlight the fundamental differences between Malachy and Angela. Malachy is impractical and idealistic; he treasures the picture because the family has managed to hold onto it during their journey from America to Ireland. Angela, on the other hand, is portrayed as being matter-of-fact and grounded, seeing the attempts to hang the portrait as a needless fuss about something unessential to their daily survival. We see these traits similarly reflected when Malachy's pride gives way to impracticality, as he refuses to pick much-needed coal off the road, telling Frank 'we're not beggars'. Angela, meanwhile, is willing to pick coal from the road and to beg at the St. Vincent de Paul Society in order to feed her family.

While anecdotes such as these are highly personal, McCourt delivers them without imposing his own voice, allowing him to comment on the social order without appearing to do so. Indeed, arguably the most significant effect of McCourt's use of anecdotes is the way in which they engage the reader emotionally with the social setting of the memoir; they draw a connection between the personal stories of the McCourts and the broader theme of life in the Lanes. McCourt's anecdotes explore the hypocrisy of the Church (for example, when Frank is rejected by the Church on the basis of his socioeconomic status), the prevalence of alcoholism (for example, when Malachy wastes his dole money on beer, forcing his wife to beg for charity lest his children starve) and the humiliation that accompanies poverty (for example, when Frank and his brother Malachy are teased at school for their shoes, which have been repaired using old tyres). Importantly, however, the majority of the anecdotes are delivered with McCourt's sense of wry humour, helping to temper and provide relief from the onslaught of misery and gloom that typifies life in poverty-stricken Limerick.

In addition to helping to structure the narrative, McCourt's use of anecdotes allows the reader to closely engage with the characters described within them, and to learn about the social setting in which characters find themselves. While McCourt refrains from imposing his own voice too strongly on these stories, he nonetheless draws in the reader to engage with his journey on a personal level; through anecdote, the reader is overwhelmed by pain when Frank is humiliated, or uplifted with joy when Frank's humanity triumphs.

REFERENCES & READING

The text

McCourt, F 2012, *Angela's Ashes*, Fourth Estate, London.

Interviews

Battersby, E 1996, 'The Great Anger', *The Irish Times*, 31 October, http://www.irishtimes.com/culture/the-great-anger-1.101226

Lamb, B 1997, 'Angela's Ashes', *Booknotes Transcript*, 31 August, http://www.booknotes.org/Watch/87803-1/Frank-McCourt

Books

Coogan, TP 1996, *Michael Collins: The Man Who Made Ireland*, Roberts Rhinehart Publishers, New York.

McCourt, M 1998, *A Monk Swimming: A Memoir*, Hyperion, New York. (This may be of use for a comparison of styles and so on, but covers a later period than that of *Angela's Ashes*.)

Royle, E 1989, *Modern Britain: A Social History 1750–1985*, Edward Arnold, London.

Swift, J 1958, 'A Modest Proposal' in *Gulliver's Travels and Other Writings*, The Modern Library, New York.

Zaczek, I 1996, *Chronicles of the Celts*, Collins & Brown Limited, London.

Film

Angela's Ashes 1999, dir. Alan Parker, Universal Studios. Starring Emily Watson, Robert Carlyle and Joe Breen.

Michael Collins 1996, dir. Neil Jordan, Warner Bros. Starring Liam Neeson, Aidan Quinn and Julia Roberts.
(Covers the period of Irish history immediately before the timespan of *Angela's Ashes*.)